THE ARCTIC OCEAN

BY JUNIATA ROGERS

NORTH AMERICA

ASIA

ARCTIC OCEAN

Published by The Child's World®
1980 Lookout Drive • Mankato, MN 56003-1705
800-599-READ • www.childsworld.com

Credits: Creative icon styles: 5 (compass); David Dennis/Shutterstock.com: 18;
Eastgreenlander/Shutterstock.com: 9; FloridaStock/Shutterstock.com: 17; Luna
Vandoorne Vallejo/Dreamstime.com: cover, 1; Steve Allen/Shutterstock.com: 10;
Tatiana Michurina/Shutterstock.com: 6; Tetyana Dotsenko/Shutterstock.com:
21; VladislavSorokin/Shutterstock.com: 13; wildestanimal/Shutterstock.com: 14

ISBN HARDCOVER: 9781503825017
ISBN PAPERBACK: 9781622434336
LCCN: 2017960227

Printed in the United States of America
PA02373

TABLE OF CONTENTS

WHERE IN THE WORLD?

Where is the Arctic Ocean? Look at the

map. Do you see North America? It is in

the west. Now look east. Find Europe and

Asia. The Arctic Ocean is above all three.

It covers the top of the world.

The Arctic Ocean is one and a
half times the size of the US.

NORTH
AMERICA

ARCTIC
OCEAN

ASIA

The Arctic Ocean is
Earth's smallest ocean.

NORTH
AMERICA

EUROPE

Some beaches along the Arctic Ocean have black sand. This beach is in Iceland.

SMALL FOR AN OCEAN

The Earth has five oceans. The Arctic

Ocean is the smallest. It is about 5.5

million square miles (14 million sq. km).

That's small for an ocean.

The Arctic Ocean mixes with the Atlantic and Pacific Oceans to its south.

FROZEN OCEAN

Sea ice covers the Arctic Ocean. In winter, sea ice is everywhere. In summer there is a lot less. Icebergs break off. They float through the water. Boats can go through the water, too.

Icebreakers are powerful ships that make paths for other boats in frozen waters.

Sea ice can have many textures.

This photo of the Arctic Ocean was taken in June—at midnight!

STRANGE DAYS

In the Arctic, summer nights are bright.

The sun stays out for weeks or months.

In winter, it is dark all day.

People call the Arctic the "Land of the Midnight Sun."

THE NORTH POLE

The **North Pole** is in the Arctic Ocean.

There is no pole to climb. There is only

ice. At the North Pole, every direction

is south!

At the North Pole, there is one sunrise and one sunset each year.

The North Pole doesn't have a time zone.

A narwhal's tusk has nerves in it.

ANIMALS OF THE ARCTIC

Is the Arctic Ocean too cold for animals?

No! Many kinds of fish and animals live

here. Crabs, lobsters, and seals live here.

So do **narwhals**. These whales have a

long, straight tooth called a **tusk**.

The lion's mane jellyfish likes Arctic waters. It grows to be about 98 feet (30 m) long.

Polar bears are the Arctic Ocean's most famous animal. They live and hunt in the ocean and nearby land areas. The bears spend most of their time on the sea ice. They hunt seals for food.

Polar bear numbers are dropping. Warmer weather, melting ice, and pollution mean trouble for polar bears.

A female polar bear is called a sow. Her baby is called a cub.

The average depth of the Arctic Ocean is 3,953 feet (1,205 m).

THE CHANGING ARCTIC

Lately, the Arctic has less ice. Scientists

are worried. Sea ice is important. It

reflects the sun. This keeps Earth cool.

With less ice, Earth might get too hot.

Litke Deep is the deepest part
of the Arctic Ocean. It is
17,880 feet (5,450 m) deep.

THE ARCTIC OCEAN'S FUTURE

The Arctic Ocean is cold. It is unusual.

It is important. We must work to keep

it healthy.

The Arctic is named for the big dipper, which is also called "big bear." *Arktos* is Greek for "bear."

There are more kinds of
fish in the Arctic Ocean
than in any other ocean.

GLOSSARY

narwhals (NAR-wallz): A narwhal is a whale that lives in the Arctic Ocean. Male narwhals have a long, straight tusk.

North Pole (NORTH POHL): The North Pole is the northernmost point on Earth. The North Pole is in the Arctic Ocean.

sea ice (SEE EYSS): Sea ice is frozen ocean water. There is more sea ice during the winter months than in the summer.

tusk (TUSK): A tusk is a long tooth that some animals have. Male narwhal whales have a tusk.

TO FIND OUT MORE

Books

Marsico, Katie. *Narwhal*. Chicago, IL: Heinemann Raintree, 2012.

Oachs, Emily Rose. *Arctic Ocean*. Minneapolis, MN: Bellwether Media. 2016.

Spilsbury, Louise, and Richard Spilsbury. *Arctic Ocean*. Chicago, IL: Heinemann Raintree, 2015.

Taylor, Barbara. *Arctic and Antarctic*. New York, NY: DK Publishing, 2012.

Web Sites

Visit our Web site for links about the Arctic Ocean:

childsworld.com/links

Note to Parents, Teachers, and Librarians: We routinely verify our Web links to make sure they are safe and active sites. So encourage your readers to check them out!

INDEX

ABOUT THE AUTHOR

Juniata Rogers grew up in Newport, RI, an island town on the Atlantic Ocean. She has worked as a naturalist, an art model, and a teacher. She's been writing professionally for 25 years, and currently lives near Washington, DC.